I THINK I CAN
I KNOW I CAN

AN
A-Z
CAREER COLORING
AND
STORY BOOK

DENISE W. THARPE

WESTBOW
PRESS®
A DIVISION OF THOMAS NELSON
& ZONDERVAN

WestBow Press books may be ordered through booksellers or by contacting:

WestBow Press
A Division of Thomas Nelson & Zondervan
1663 Liberty Drive
Bloomington, IN 47403
www.westbowpress.com
1 (866) 928-1240

ISBN: 978-1-9736-9383-3 (sc)
ISBN: 978-1-9736-9382-6 (e)

Print information available on the last page.

WestBow Press rev. date: 6/9/2020

Bible Scripture: Phil 4;13 I can do all things through Christ who give me strength.

ASTRONAUT

My name is _____

I want to be an astronaut because an astronaut is a person who is trained to travel into outer space, and visit many planets.

DRAWING PAGE

BASKETBALL PLAYER

My name is _____

I would like to be a Basketball player. Although it can be a hobby, it can also turn into a productive career. Basketball is a team sport with 5 players on each team competing to shoot the ball into the hoop to determine who wins the game.

BASKETBALL

DRAWING PAGE

CONSTRUCTION WORKER

My name is _____

I want to be a construction worker because I like to build! A construction worker builds homes, tall buildings, roads, railroad and even schools.

DRAWING PAGE

DOCTOR

My name is _____

I want to be a Doctor so that I can help people when they are sick. Doctors are very important people in the world who are trained to help the sick get well.

DRAWING PAGE

ENGINEER

My name is _____

I would like to be an engineer, an engineer is a person who designs, builds, or fixes engines, machines, or public works.

ENGINEER

DRAWING PAGE

FIREFIGHTER

My name is _____

I would like to be a firefighter to help save lives. A firefighter is a person who is trained on how to put out fires, large or small.

DRAWING PAGE

GARDNER

My name is _____

I want to be a Gardner because I love being in the outdoors planting and seeing beautiful things grow like beautiful plants, flowers, and vegetables.

DRAWING PAGE

HANDY MAN

My name is _____

I want to be a handyman because I like fixing things that are broken. A handy man fixes appliances like Refrigerators, stoves and many more things.

DRAWING PAGE

INSPECTOR

My name is _____

I want to be an inspector, I like to solve mysteries and unsolved stories. An inspector is a person who is trained to inspect something or someone.

DRAWING PAGE

JUDGE

My name is _____

I would like to one day become a Judge. Judges are people who have been appointed to decide cases in the court of law.

DRAWING PAGE

KINDERGARTEN TEACHER

My name is _____

I want to be a Kindergarten Teacher to help children learn like my teacher helped me learn. A Kindergarten Teacher is a person who teaches in a school setting. They prepare children for the higher grades of elementary school.

DRAWING PAGE

LIBRARIAN

My name is _____

I want to be a Librarian, I love to read books and learn about different things. A Librarian is a person who is trained and in charge of working in a library setting.

LiBRARiAN

LIBRARIAN

DRAWING PAGE

MAKE-UP-ARTIST

My name is _____

I want to be a Makeup Artist because I like to make people look good. A makeup artist uses their tools to improve and enhance a person's face.

DRAWING PAGE

NURSE

My name is _____

I want to be a Nurse so that I can help someone who is sick. A Nurse a person who is trained to assist the Doctor in taking care of a person who is sick, in a doctor's office or hospital.

DRAWING PAGE

OPTOMETRIST

My name is _____

I want to be an Optometrist to help people see better. An Optometrist is a person who practices eye and vision care to help others see better.

OPTOMETRIST

DRAWING PAGE

PEST CONTROL WORKER

My name is _____

I want to be a Pest Control Worker so that I can help keep the bugs away. The Pest Control Worker helps remove and control insects and rodents from homes and businesses.

DRAWING PAGE

QUEEN

My name is _____

I want to be a Queen one day to be a ruler over a country. Most Queens are inherited in their position. They are the ruler over their Independent State and are very powerful people.

DRAWING PAGE

RECEPTION

My name is _____

I want to be a Reception to help customers with their needs. A Receptionist is a person that works in an office setting to help clients and answer the phone.

RECEPTION

DRAWING PAGE

SECRETARY

My name is _____

I want to be a secretary to take care of office needs.

A Secretary is responsible for working in an office to assist with correspondence, keep records, make appointments, and carry out similar tasks.

SECRETARY

DRAWING PAGE

TEACHER

My name is _____

I want to be a Teacher to help students to learn. A Teacher is a person who is trained to teach students and help them to acquire knowledge.

TEACHER

DRAWING PAGE

ULTRASOUND DOCTOR

My name is _____

I want to be an Ultrasound Doctor to help people see what they otherwise could not see through and Ultrasound Machine. An Ultrasound Doctor is a trained person who uses an Ultrasound to make a diagnosis and determine the best results.

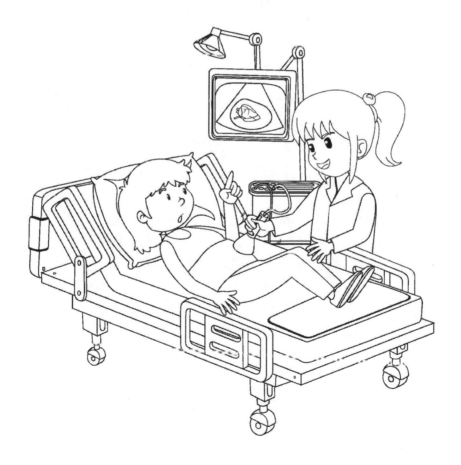

DRAWING PAGE

VETERINARIAN

My name is _____

I want to be a Veterinarian because I love animals.

A Veterinarian is a person who is trained to treat and take care of all types of animals.

VETERINARIAN

DRAWING PAGE

WOMAN SCIENTIST

My name is _____

I want to be a Woman Scientist to help change the world for the better. A Woman Scientist is a person who has expert knowledge of natural or physical science.

DRAWING PAGE

X- RAY DOCTOR

My name is _____

I want to be an X-Ray Doctor to help people and examine their body to see if something is wrong.

An X-Ray Doctor uses x-ray equipment to see and examine your body to make a diagnosis, so that they can determine how to get results.

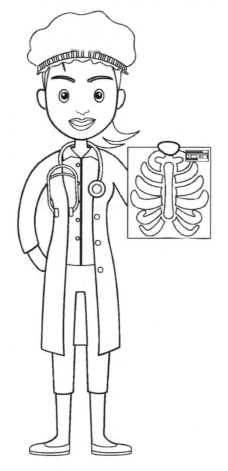

DRAWING PAGE

YARD KEEPER

My name is _____

I want to be a Yard Keeper because I like being outdoors. A Yard Keeper is a person that is responsible for keeping the yard in good shape also, making sure that the flowers and plants, gardens and trees are all well taken care of.

YARD KEEPER

DRAWING PAGE

ZOOKEEPER

My name is _____

I want to be a Zookeeper because I love animals.

A Zookeeper is a person who cares for animals in the Zoo.

Printed in the United States
By Bookmasters